Jesus Has Come

A FAMILY DEVOTIONAL ON GOD'S PROMISES FULFILLED

THE DAILY GRACE CO.

In this study

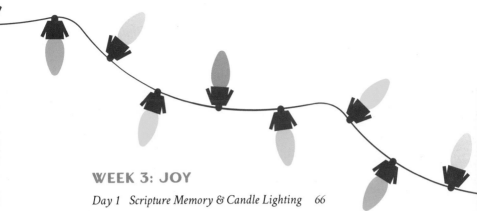

Hey, Grown-Ups!

We are thrilled that you have chosen *Jesus Has Come: A Family Devotional on God's Promises Fulfilled* as part of your Advent celebration this year. This devotional is crafted to help everyone in your home remember that Jesus is the true reason we celebrate Christmas.

HOW TO USE THIS DEVOTIONAL

This resource contains four weeks of daily devotional content, and it begins on the fourth Sunday before Christmas. We suggest allowing 10-15 minutes to complete each day with your family. Each week will focus on one of the Advent candle themes: hope, peace, joy, and love. The devotions will trace that theme through the story of Scripture — from creation to the birth of Jesus to our hope of being with Jesus in eternity. A story of Scripture timeline on page 8 may be helpful to refer to as you complete each devotion.

The first day of each week is a candle lighting day (see pages 10-11 for more information on the candle lighting tradition), followed by five days of devotional content. The final day of each week provides an optional family activity. For planning purposes, on the next page is a list of supplies you will need for each of the four family activities. Some weeks you may be busier than others, so use the activities as they fit for your family.

BEFORE YOU BEGIN

You may want to spend some time discussing what Advent is with your family before you begin this devotional. You can find more information about the origin and importance of Advent on page 10.

We pray this resource illuminates the gift of Jesus for each member of your family this holiday season. May it bring you great delight in seeing God's goodness and grace toward us displayed through sending His Son, and may the eyes and hearts of your family members be opened to the good news of the gospel.

Family Activity
SUPPLY LISTS

SUPPLIES FOR ADVENT CANDLE LIGHTING

- ☐ Advent wreath (optional)
- ☐ Five candles
- ☐ Traditionally, there are three purple candles for peace, joy, and love; one pink candle for hope; and one white candle representing the Christ candle. However, feel free to use whatever candles you have around the house.

WEEK I

- ☐ Pen
- ☐ Paper
- ☐ 3 cups dry milk powder
- ☐ ½ cup unsweetened cocoa powder
- ☐ ½ cup sugar
- ☐ ¼ tsp salt
- ☐ Peppermint sticks, marshmallows, or other toppings (optional)
- ☐ Blender (optional)

WEEK 2

- ☐ White construction paper
- ☐ Pencils
- ☐ Scissors
- ☐ Glue
- ☐ Ribbon
- ☐ Hole punch
- ☐ Markers or colored pencils (optional)

WEEK 3

- ☐ Scissors
- ☐ Cardstock (any color)
- ☐ Glitter
- ☐ Sequins
- ☐ Glue
- ☐ Washable paint
- ☐ Paintbrushes
- ☐ Sticky tack

WEEK 4

Supplies needed will vary. See page 114.

WHAT IS THE STORY OF SCRIPTURE?

The Bible tells many smaller stories that make up one big story—how God is saving, redeeming, and restoring the whole world from sin and death. This devotional traces the themes of hope, peace, joy, and love throughout the big story of Scripture.

CREATION

In the beginning, God created the entire universe. He made the world and everything in it, like the animals and the trees. Most of all, He created humans like you and me.

FALL

The first humans God created were Adam and Eve. God commanded Adam and Eve not to eat the fruit from the Tree of Knowledge of Good and Evil. Because of their disobedience, sin came into the world. The punishment for sin is death, and because of Adam and Eve's sin, all humans are sinful and deserve the punishment of death. But God had a plan to send His Son Jesus to save sinful humans from this punishment.

PROPHECIES

God formed a people for Himself called the Israelites. Like Adam and Eve, the Israelites were to love and obey God. Sadly, they often disobeyed His commands. During a time when they were really sinful, God used prophets (people God chose to share His message with others) to warn the Israelites of the punishment of their sin. But God also used prophets to bring words of hope to Israel—promises of how God would send them a Savior who would bring them rescue and restoration.

Below is a timeline and a brief overview of the story of Scripture. See if you can spot these parts of the story of Scripture in your devotions each week!

THE BIRTH OF JESUS

This promised Savior was Jesus! He was born as a small baby in a little town called Bethlehem.

JESUS'S DEATH AND RESURRECTION

Jesus grew up and lived a sinless life. He died on the cross to pay the punishment for our sin. But He did not stay dead! Jesus rose from the grave and went back to heaven. Anyone who believes in Jesus is saved from the punishment of their sin and given eternal life with God.

JESUS'S SECOND COMING

One day, Jesus will return to restore the world to a place without sin. All of God's people will live with God forever.

ETERNITY FUTURE

What is Advent?

Do you ever have a hard time remembering?
Maybe you have forgotten to put away your dirty socks
or accidentally left a school assignment at home. We all
forget sometimes. We can even forget that Christmas is
not just about presents, cookies, and pretty twinkling lights.
These are all fun and wonderful, but Christmas is about
someone much more important—Jesus!

Jesus left His perfect home in heaven to come to earth and be with us. He even chose to come in a special way—as a little, tiny baby! Christmas is a celebration of the day He was born. Jesus came to show the world what God is like and how big His love is. The biggest way He showed God's love was by dying on the cross to pay for the sins of the world. Jesus's arrival is so important that we never want to forget it!

Advent helps us think about the importance of Jesus every day leading up to Christmas. Advent comes from the Latin word meaning "coming or arrival." Every Advent devotion in this book is meant to help you remember the day Jesus came as a baby and look forward to the day He will come to the earth again in the future. Remembering Jesus is the most important thing we can do, and Advent helps us do just that!

Many, many years ago, people decided to celebrate the birth of Jesus by lighting candles each day during Advent. The light of the candles lit up the darkness the same way Jesus lights up the world with His love and truth. The candles were often placed on a wreath, which is a circle. Circles have no beginning and no end, just like God! He has always been and always will be. The Advent candle lighting tradition is just another way to remind ourselves how important Jesus is in our lives.

WEEK 1

Hope

MEMORY VERSE

This hope will not disappoint us, because God's love has been poured out in our hearts through the Holy Spirit who was given to us.

Romans 5:5

MEMORY VERSE MEMORY VERSE MEMORY VERSE MEMORY VERSE MEMORY VERSE

WEEK 1 - DAY 1

Read John 16:22, 2 Corinthians 4:16-18

Hope

Today, we will light the hope candle. Hope is believing that there are better things ahead. Even when we experience hard or sad things, the hope of Jesus lights our lives. All those who believe in Jesus have the hope of being saved from sin, experiencing the help and comfort of the Holy Spirit, and looking forward to eternity with Jesus, which will be free from sin and sadness. As you light the hope candle today, read the verses above, and reflect on the present and future hope we have in Jesus.

PRAYER

God,

When we feel sad, disappointed, or hurt, help us to remember that this is not the end of the story. Jesus came to bring the hope that we have now, which lasts forever. No matter what, the hope Jesus gives to us cannot be taken away. He has saved us from our sins and promised to spend eternity with us in a perfect paradise. Thank You for this wonderful truth! We have so much to look forward to! Help us put our hope in You and Your promises alone.

Amen.

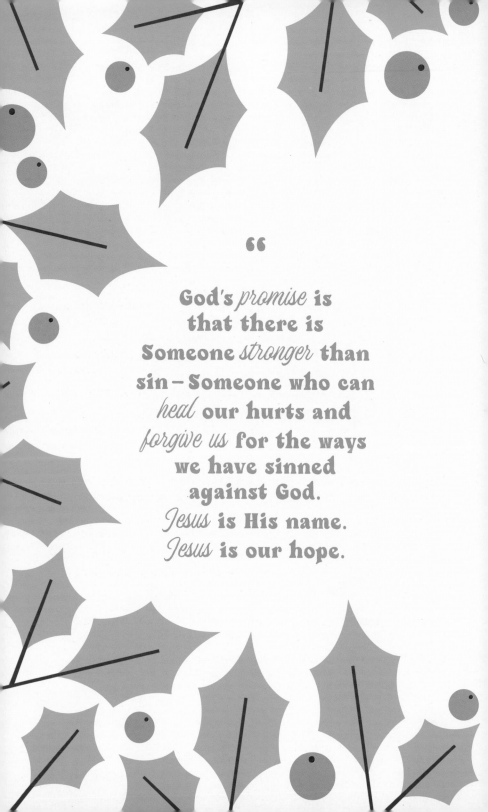

"

God's *promise* is
that there is
Someone *stronger* than
sin — Someone who can
heal our hurts and
forgive us for the ways
we have sinned
against God.
Jesus is His name.
Jesus is our hope.

Hope in Creation

READ TOGETHER: GENESIS 2:15-17,
GENESIS 3:2-7, GENESIS 3:13-15

When God created the world, it was beautiful and full of His presence. He created two very special people, Adam and Eve, to live in and enjoy the garden of Eden. They could go anywhere in the garden and do anything. Except for one thing—they were not to eat from the tree at the center of the garden. That tree, God said, was not good for them to eat.

Suddenly, a snake enters the story. He is not an ordinary snake. He is Satan, the enemy of God. Satan's only goal is to separate people from God. He convinced Adam and Eve to eat the fruit God asked them to avoid. Satan told them the fruit was good, but Adam and Eve knew the serpent lied as soon as they ate it. They had disobeyed God; they had sinned. And because of this, there were consequences.

God sent Adam and Eve out of the garden. Their lives would be harder now, and they would be separated from Him. But even at this moment, when their bad decision was causing them so much pain, God gave them a promise to hold onto with hope. One day, the serpent would be defeated once and for all. Though their sin caused pain and heartache, someday a Savior would take all pain, sin, and sorrow away forever, and people would be able to come close to God again.

We sin, too. And sometimes, we experience hurt when others sin against us. God's promise is that there is Someone stronger than sin—Someone who can heal our hurts and forgive us for the ways we have sinned against God. Jesus is His name. Jesus is our hope.

ANSWER TOGETHER

What is sin? Do you ever sin?

Hint: 1 John 3:4, James 1:14-15, Romans 3:23

We all sin, and sin separates us from God.
But even though we are sinners, we have hope in Jesus
because He forgives the sins of those who believe in Him.
What do you think it means to believe in Jesus?

Hint: Romans 10:9 and Romans 5:1

PRAY TOGETHER

✝ *Ask God to forgive you of the sins you*
have committed.

✝ *Thank God that He gives hope through*
Jesus to everyone who sins.

draw a picture
ABOUT WHAT YOU LEARNED TODAY

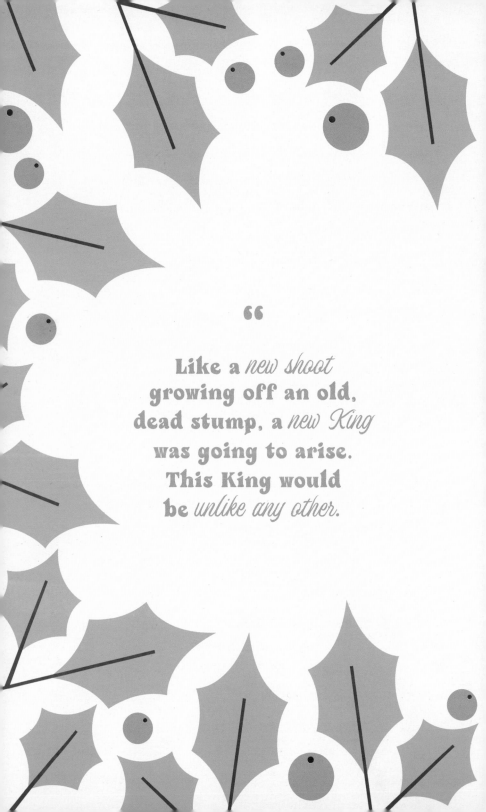

"

Like a *new shoot*
growing off an old,
dead stump, a *new King*
was going to arise.
This King would
be *unlike any other.*

Hope Promised

READ TOGETHER: ISAIAH 11:1-5

How do you feel when you have to wait for something? Excited? Frustrated? Worried? Yesterday, we talked about God's promise of a Savior who would save the world from sin. God's people were really, really excited for the promised Savior to arrive, but they had to wait a long, long time. There were hundreds of years between God's promise to Adam and Eve and when Jesus finally arrived.

In this time of waiting, sin was a big problem. People chose not to listen to God and did things God said not to do. People were angry and mean and hateful. All of this made God really sad. He kept having to give His children consequences for their disobedience.

Even though these were some dark days, God still wanted His people to see how hope was lighting up their future. He gave them another promise. He said their nation was like an empty field right now, and nothing good was growing from it. But one day, something new was going to grow from the emptiness. Like a new shoot growing off an old, dead stump, a new King was going to arise. This King would be unlike any other. He would be faithful to God and never sin. He would be wise and kind and just, too. And this King would lead God's people to love and obey God.

All the people rejoiced at these hopeful words! This is the King they wanted and needed. Their hope was renewed, and they held onto this hope tightly as they continued to wait for their King, who we know as Jesus.

ANSWER TOGETHER

*Even when God's people were disobeying and He had
to give them consequences, He also encouraged them
with the hope that a Savior was coming.*
Why do you think God did this?
What does this tell us about God?

*We may face times when people let us down
like the leaders of God's people let them
down by disobeying Him.*
Has this ever happened to you?
Could Jesus be your hope in these hard times
like He was the hope for God's people?

PRAY TOGETHER

✠ *Ask God to help you wait in areas you
are feeling impatient.*

✠ *Thank God for promising King Jesus who
would lead people to love and obey God.*

draw a picture
ABOUT WHAT YOU LEARNED TODAY

66

Jesus's **birth was all about** *hope*.

Hope in the Birth of Jesus

READ TOGETHER: MATTHEW 1:18-21

Grown-ups: Consider showing children pictures of themselves as a baby or young child before starting today's devotion.

Every baby is special. Each one is born with unique features and personalities. Maybe you were born with dark, curly hair or no hair at all. Maybe you have freckles, a sweet button nose, or an extra big space between your toes. These are the things that make you… you!

Jesus was the most special baby of all. We do not know the color of His hair or if He was tall or small. But we know He was special because He is the only baby ever born who was also God. He was not just a nice man and a wise teacher; He was called "Immanuel," which means "God with us." We cannot see God, and sometimes, it is hard to hear His voice. Thankfully, Jesus is God, and He was born to be with people on earth. People saw what Jesus did and heard what He said. Through Jesus, they saw who God is and what He is like. And they wrote down many stories about Jesus, which are recorded in the Bible.

Jesus's birth was all about hope. He was the hope all the world had been waiting for. And they had waited a long time for Jesus. The day He was born, the waiting was over. Hope had come. He was right there, laying in the manger, and Jesus would live His whole life to show people God was good and faithful and true and that it was good to hope in Him!

JESUS WOULD LIVE HIS WHOLE LIFE
TO SHOW PEOPLE GOD WAS GOOD
AND FAITHFUL AND TRUE.

What makes Jesus different from
any other baby ever born?

*Immanuel is one of Jesus's names.
It means "God with us."*
What do you think it means that
Jesus is God with us?

✚ *Ask God to help you understand the
messages about God that Jesus came to bring.*

✚ *Thank God for fulfilling His promise and
sending Jesus to be your hope.*

draw a picture

ABOUT WHAT YOU LEARNED TODAY

"

Jesus's death
was *not the end* of
His story – it was
the way through
which He forgave the
sins of the world.

Hope in Jesus's Death and Resurrection

READ TOGETHER: MATTHEW 28:5-7

After Jesus was born, God's people could not wait for Him to be the King and make all the wrong things right—just like God promised. But Jesus sure was an odd King. He did not live in a palace or wear a crown. He lived in a small house in a quiet town, and He was a carpenter just like His earthly father, Joseph. Some people even began to think He was not the Savior King after all. Other people believed Jesus when He said He was the Savior sent by God.

Then, things got even more confusing because, after only a few years of Jesus showing God's love and grace to people, Jesus was hung on a cross, and He died. How could He ever be a King now that He was gone? People believed hope was gone now that Jesus was buried. But the most amazing thing happened after Jesus had been dead for three days. He rose back to life! Jesus's friends saw His empty tomb, and then, they saw Him walking and talking with them! How could this be? It was a miracle!

Jesus's death was not the end of His story—it was the way through which He forgave the sins of the world. All people deserve death as the consequence of sin, but Jesus died in our place. Only, He did not stay dead, but He rose again! He defeated sin and death forever so that those who believe in Him can live with Him forever. Jesus truly is the Savior King, yet He saved the world on the cross and not from a palace. We all have the hope of forgiveness for our sins through the death and resurrection of Jesus. Jesus is our hope!

*When Jesus died, God's people doubted if
He really was the Savior King.*
Do you ever doubt that Jesus can help and save you?

Jesus's death paid for our sins. This good news
is called the gospel. Practice saying the gospel
message out loud to your family.
It could sound something like:

*I am a sinner, and the consequence of my sin was death.
Jesus died to pay the consequence of my sin, so I do not
have to. If I believe in Jesus, ask Him to forgive my sins,
and pursue a relationship with Him, I will not die but
will spend eternity with Him in heaven.*

+ *Ask God to help you remember the hope of
Jesus in good times and bad.*

+ *Thank Jesus for paying the price for your
sins on the cross.*

ABOUT WHAT YOU LEARNED TODAY

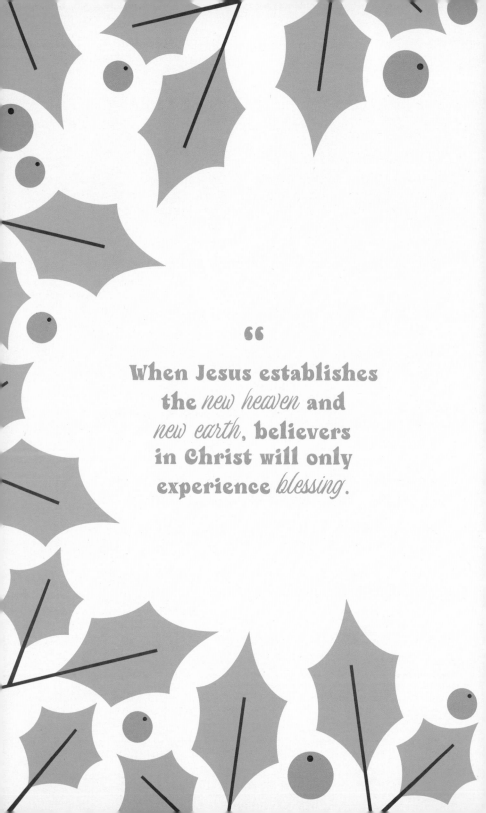

"

When Jesus establishes
the *new heaven* and
new earth, believers
in Christ will only
experience *blessing*.

Hope in The Second Coming of Jesus

READ TOGETHER: REVELATION 21:3-4

Did you know God's story of bringing hope to the world is still being written? It is true! Jesus came to the earth once, but He is also coming again one day. We do not know when this day will be, but we know what will happen on that day. Jesus will get rid of all sin, pain, and sadness. He will make everything right that sin has made wrong. He will also get rid of Satan, so he can never tempt anyone to sin ever again. And Jesus will reign over the earth as the Savior King forever.

Everyone who believes in Jesus will live in this wonderful, perfect world with Him. Can you imagine that? No more tears! No more bad days! No more waiting for Jesus because He will be with us forevermore. But that day has not come yet, so we are waiting right now. And we wait with hope. He came before just as He said, and He will come again just as He promised.

Titus 2:13 calls Jesus's second coming our "blessed hope," which means this hope is one that will bring blessings. The biblical definition of "blessed" is "to be in God's grace and favor." Those in Christ experience God's grace and favor now, but they also experience the effects of sin. When Jesus establishes the new heaven and new earth, believers in Christ will only experience blessing. This truth gives us hope that no matter what happens in our lives, we have something good to look forward to in eternity with Jesus!

ANSWER TOGETHER

*Consider how we have traced the theme
of hope throughout Scripture from
Genesis to Revelation this week.*
What have you learned about God's story
of hope from studying in this way?

Why are you looking forward to
the second coming of Jesus?

PRAY TOGETHER

+ *Tell Jesus you are waiting with hope for
the day He comes again.*

+ *Thank God for being trustworthy and
always keeping His promises.*

draw a picture
ABOUT WHAT YOU LEARNED TODAY

Family Hot Cocoa Night

SUPPLIES NEEDED

Pen
Paper
Ingredients for Hot Cocoa Recipe
Optional Hot Cocoa Toppings

HOT COCOA RECIPE

3 cups dry milk powder
½ cup unsweetened cocoa powder
½ cup sugar
¼ tsp salt

Place all ingredients in a blender, and blend until it is a fine powder. Alternatively, mix all ingredients well in a bowl if you do not have a blender. Next, boil water or warm it to the desired temperature. Then, place ¼ cup in a coffee mug or tea cup, and mix 8 oz of boiling water to make cocoa. Optional: Add peppermint sticks, marshmallows, whipped cream, or chocolate shavings.

Enjoy sipping cocoa while you make a list of holiday activities your family looks forward to during the weeks leading up to Christmas. The list could include anything from decorating a Christmas tree to opening gifts to spending time with relatives.

Discuss how each of these things reminds us to remember the hope we have in Jesus — both to save us from our sins and to redeem the whole earth when He comes again.

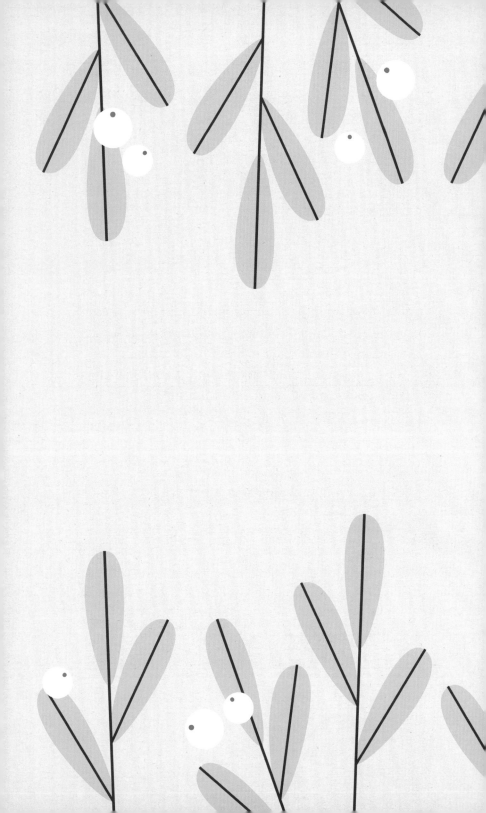

WEEK 2

Peace

MEMORY VERSE

For a child will be born for us, a son will be given to us, and the government will be on his shoulders. He will be named Wonderful Counselor, Mighty God, Eternal Father, Prince of Peace.

Isaiah 9:6

MEMORY VERSE MEMORY VERSE MEMORY VERSE MEMORY VERSE MEMORY VERSE

WEEK 2 - DAY 1

Read Luke 2:14, Romans 5:1

Peace

Today, we light the peace candle. The peace candle is called the angel's candle because it reminds us of the peace the angels proclaimed when Jesus was born. When we think of peace, we might think of a time when no fighting is happening—but God's peace is so much more! The grace and forgiveness we can receive through Jesus mends the broken relationship between God and us, resulting in peace. We may live in a world where sad things happen today, but the peace candle reminds us how peace has come to earth through Christ and how peace will fully come to earth when Christ returns and sets all things right. As you light the peace candle today, read the verses above, and reflect on the peace Jesus brings.

PRAYER

Dear God,

Our world can feel dark because of how people hurt one another and refuse to forgive. As we light this candle, help us to remember that You are our God of peace. Help us to remember that You sent Jesus, our Prince of Peace, to bring us true and lasting peace. We praise You for how the peace of Christ breaks through the darkness of this world. May we rest in the peace of Christ when we feel sad and afraid, and may we look to the day when we will experience a world of complete and everlasting harmony with You.

Amen

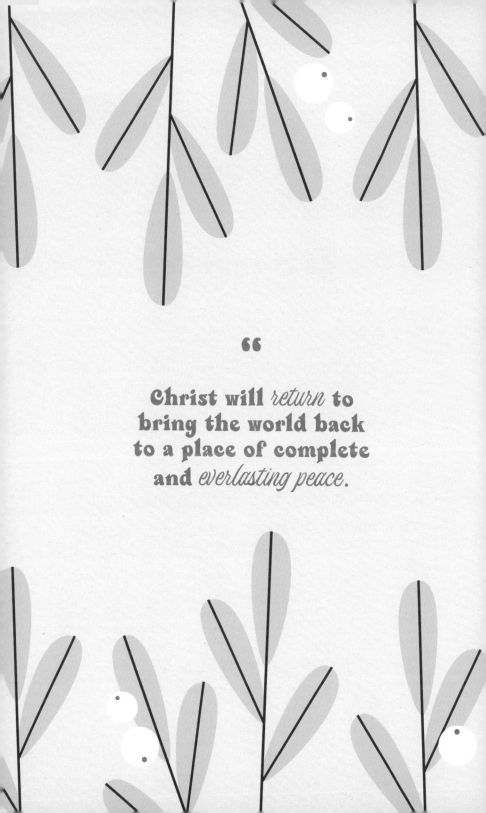

"

Christ will *return* to
bring the world back
to a place of complete
and *everlasting peace*.

Peace in Creation

READ TOGETHER: GENESIS 1:28-31, GENESIS 3:15

God created the world to be a place of peace. Everything God made was good, which means that all of creation lived in perfect harmony. Animals were kind to each other, and humans were kind to animals and one another. Best of all, humans had a relationship with God that was perfect. Can you imagine a world like this? It would be a place with no bullies or fights with siblings. There would be no chaotic storms or bad things that hurt people or made them sad.

This was the world God created, but sadly, this all changed when Adam and Eve sinned. Adam and Eve's sin broke the perfect peace of creation. Sin creates conflict and brings back the chaos God put into order. Sin also hurts our relationship with God. In the place of peace with God, we now experience the wrath of God because sin deserves to be punished.

But God is a good and faithful God, and He will not allow His creation to remain broken. God put forth a plan to send His Son, Jesus, to repair the world's brokenness. Mankind cannot restore peace, but Jesus can. The sacrifice Jesus made on the cross restores those who believe in Jesus back to a right relationship with God. Because of Christ's forgiveness, those who have a relationship with Jesus have peace with God once again. And one day, Christ will return to bring the world back to a place of complete and everlasting peace.

GOD IS A GOOD AND FAITHFUL GOD.

ANSWER TOGETHER

What are some ways you see a lack of peace
in the world today?

What does it say about God's character that
He wants to restore perfect peace?

PRAY TOGETHER

✚ *Thank God for sending Jesus to
give us peace.*

✚ *Thank God for how He will restore
perfect peace one day through Jesus.*

draw a picture
ABOUT WHAT YOU LEARNED TODAY

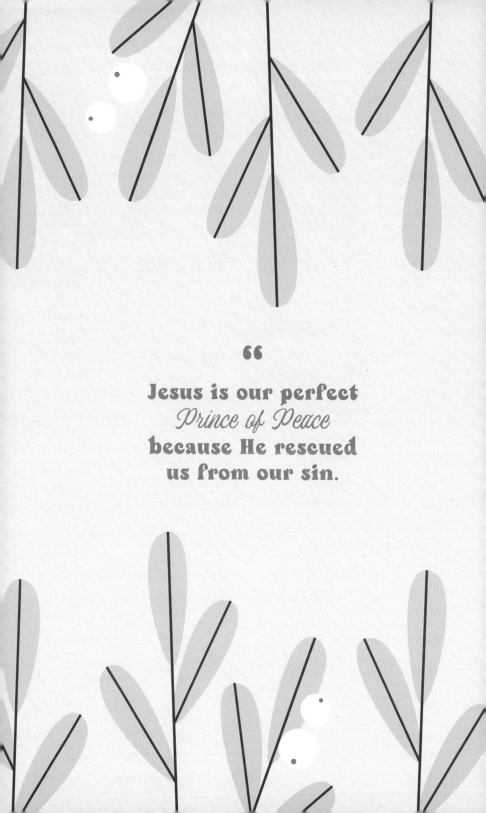

66

Jesus is our perfect
Prince of Peace
because He rescued
us from our sin.

Peace Promised

READ TOGETHER: ISAIAH 9:6-7, ISAIAH 53:5

Do you have a favorite story about a prince or princess? It is magical to see or read about a prince riding in on his horse to save the damsel in distress. Advent is a season of waiting, and just like a princess waiting for rescue, we too are waiting to be rescued. God's plan to send Jesus is a plan of rescue to save sinners from the punishment of their sin.

In the Old Testament, God used prophets to explain His promise to His chosen people, who are called the Israelites. One of these prophecies told how a Prince of Peace would come to Israel. Isaiah 9 tells us how this Prince of Peace would reign as a righteous ruler and build an eternal kingdom of peace. This Prince of Peace is Jesus.

The word for "peace" in Isaiah 9 is the word *shâlôwm*. This *shâlôwm* peace means to fix what is broken, particularly the broken relationship sin caused between God and man. Jesus is our perfect Prince of Peace because He rescued us from our sin. Isaiah 53:5 tells us how Jesus took on the punishment of our sin on the cross so we could have peace. The grace of Christ puts the broken pieces of our relationship with God back together. Our Prince of Peace has rescued us from the punishment of our sin, and He will come again to give us full rescue when He cleanses the world from sin once and for all.

OUR PRINCE OF PEACE HAS RESCUED US FROM THE PUNISHMENT OF OUR SIN.

ANSWER TOGETHER

How would the promised Prince of Peace
encourage Israel while they waited?

How does God sending Jesus to rescue
us show His love for us?

PRAY TOGETHER

✝ *Praise Jesus for being our Prince of Peace.*

✝ *Ask God to help you remember the
sacrifice Jesus made to give us His peace.*

draw a picture
ABOUT WHAT YOU LEARNED TODAY

66

May this *Advent*
season encourage you
to *rest* **in the only**
One who can give us
peace, **Jesus Christ.**

Peace in the Birth of Jesus

READ TOGETHER: LUKE 2:1-14, JOHN 14:27

Christmas is a time to celebrate the birth of the Prince of Peace. The promise spoken to Israel about a Prince of Peace was fulfilled through the birth of Christ. On the night of Christ's birth, angels appeared to a group of shepherds and sang how peace had come to earth. Luke 2:14 tells us that this peace is given to people God favors.

What does this mean? We learned yesterday that *shâlôwm* peace is made possible only through Jesus Christ. The only way we can experience God's peace is to have a relationship with God, given to us through Jesus. True and lasting peace is found in Christ alone.

If we look at our world today, we can see how many people do not know God's peace. Many people purposefully hurt one another and fight with one another. It can be sad to see how the world is without peace—but there is hope! Believers today continue to experience God's peace through God's Holy Spirit. The Holy Spirit dwells inside believers, which means all believers have the peaceful presence of God with them every day.

Whenever we feel scared or sad, we can come to Jesus. John 14:27 says that Jesus's peace is different than the world's peace. Jesus's peace is different from the peace the world offers because Jesus's peace stays with us, even if we do not always feel it. May this Advent season encourage you to rest in the only One who can give us peace, Jesus Christ.

ALL BELIEVERS HAVE THE PEACEFUL PRESENCE OF GOD WITH THEM EVERY DAY.

ANSWER TOGETHER

What do you turn to for peace?

How does knowing Jesus is the true source
of peace encourage you to come to Him?

PRAY TOGETHER

✝ *Thank Jesus for being our source of
true and lasting peace.*

✝ *Pray that God will help you remember
to go to Jesus when you need peace.*

draw a picture

ABOUT WHAT YOU LEARNED TODAY

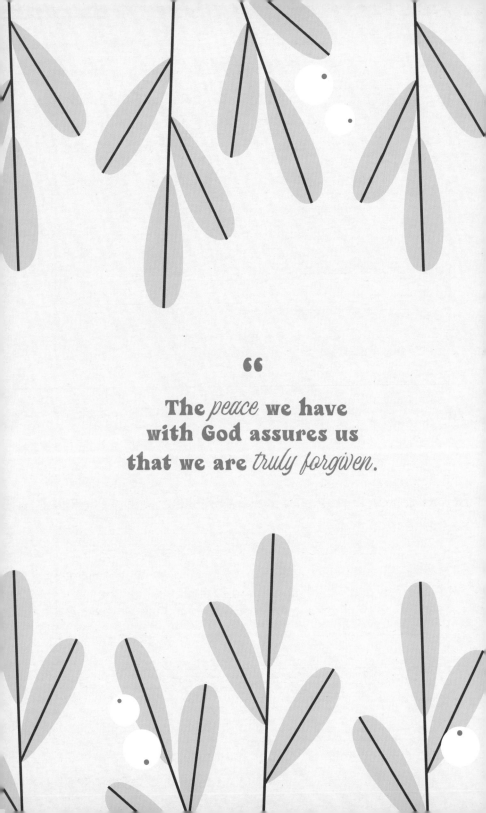

66

The *peace* we have
with God assures us
that we are *truly forgiven.*

Peace in Jesus's Death and Resurrection

READ TOGETHER: ROMANS 5:1

Think of a time when you had a disagreement with a sibling or friend. Whether they did something to upset you or you did something to upset them, your conflict hurt your relationship. There needed to be forgiveness for that broken relationship to be restored.

Because of sin, every person is in conflict with God. Unlike our relationships with others, there is nothing we can do on our own to fix our relationship with God. But that is why God sent Jesus! Romans 5:1 tells us that we have peace with God because of Christ. Christ's forgiveness restores our once-broken relationship with God. This is the beauty of the gospel!

Because of Christ's sacrifice, there is no longer any wrath between God and us. This means we don't have to be afraid to confess our sins to God! The peace we have with God assures us that we are truly forgiven.

Our peace with God encourages us to share God's peace with others. We share God's peace by being kind to others but also by sharing the gospel. Second Corinthians 5:19 tells us that we have been given the message of reconciliation to share. "Reconciliation" means "a restored relationship with God," which is something we should want all people to have.

This Advent season is an opportunity to share with others the peace they can have through Christ. Let us respond to the peace we have received through Christ by sharing Christ's peace with others!

ANSWER TOGETHER

Who can you share the gospel with
this Advent season?

How can you be a person of peace this season?

PRAY TOGETHER

✚ *Thank Jesus for being the One who
reconciles us to God.*

✚ *Ask God to give you opportunities to share
the message of Christ's peace this season.*

draw a picture
ABOUT WHAT YOU LEARNED TODAY

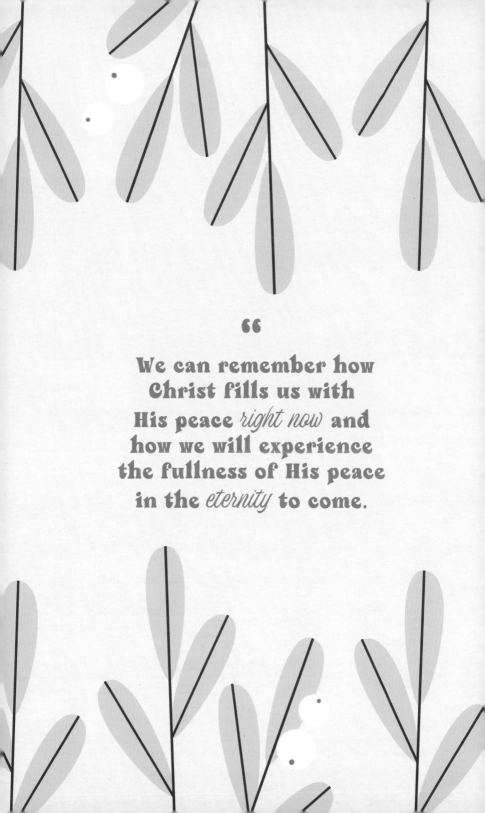

"

We can remember how
Christ fills us with
His peace *right now* and
how we will experience
the fullness of His peace
in the *eternity* to come.

Peace in the Second Coming of Jesus

READ TOGETHER: REVELATION 21:1-4, JOHN 16:33

Advent helps us anticipate the birth of Christ. This season of waiting gives us excitement and joy as we count down to Christmas day. But the Advent season also teaches us to anticipate the second advent—when Christ returns!

Revelation 21 paints us a beautiful picture of what it will be like when Christ returns. In Revelation 21:5, God says, "Look, I am making everything new." This means that the whole world will be made new by the removal of sin. All brokenness and sin will be washed from the earth, resulting in all of creation being good once again.

Revelation 21:4 tells us, "He will wipe away every tear from their eyes. Death will be no more; grief, crying, and pain will be no more, because the previous things have passed away." Picture someone who loves and cares for you wiping your tears after you skinned your knee. This picture is what God will do for every person who has a relationship with Christ. God will wipe away everything that gives us a lack of peace today.

What a happy day that will be! But what does that mean for us right now? John 16:33 says that in Christ we have peace. Even though we live in a world of sadness and sin, we can rest in our Prince of Peace. When the waiting feels long, we can remember how Christ fills us with His peace right now and how we will experience the fullness of His peace in the eternity to come.

*Consider how we have traced the theme of peace
throughout Scripture from Genesis to Revelation this week.*
What have you learned about God's story of
peace from studying in this way?

How does knowing Christ will return give you hope?

✝ *Praise Jesus for how He will make all
things new.*

✝ *Ask God to help you rest in His peace
as you wait for Jesus's return.*

draw a picture
ABOUT WHAT YOU LEARNED TODAY

Make a Dove Ornament

SUPPLIES NEEDED

White construction paper
Pencils
Scissors
Glue
Ribbon
Hole punch
Markers or colored pencils (optional)

INSTRUCTIONS

Doves have been used as symbols of peace for centuries. Follow the directions below to make your own dove ornament that can remind you of the peace Jesus brings.

Use the dove stencil on the next page to trace a dove on your white construction paper. Cut out the traced dove with scissors. Add any details you would like on your dove, such as feathers, an eye, or you can even write the word "peace" if you would like! Use a hole punch to punch a hole in the paper. Thread a ribbon through the hole, and tie it with a knot. Hang it on your tree!

FAMILY ACTIVITY FAMILY ACTIVITY FAMILY ACTIVITY FAMILY

WEEK 3

JOY

MEMORY VERSE

You reveal the path of life to me; in your presence is abundant joy; at your right hand are eternal pleasures.

Psalm 16:11

WEEK 3 - DAY 1

Read Psalm 100, Philippians 4:4-5

Joy

Today, we will light the joy candle. Joy is more than just feeling happy. Joy is knowing deep in our hearts that even when we experience hard things, Jesus promises to be with us, help us, and forgive us. He also promises that life won't always be hard—one day, we will be with Him, experiencing a peace that never ends! These promises mean we can have joy no matter what. Joy in Jesus lights up our hearts and makes us glad! As you light the joy candle today, read the verses above, and reflect on the present and future joy we have in Jesus.

PRAYER

God,

Sometimes life is happy, and sometimes it is sad, but no matter what, we always have joy in You. Would You help us remember this? And would You remind us of the joy we will experience in eternity with You? Help us to be people of joy, spreading joy to those around us this holiday season.

Amen.

> *Jesus* was God's
> ultimate plan to bring
> *joy* to the earth.

Joy in Creation

READ TOGETHER: GENESIS 1:31

Have you ever created something you were very proud of? Maybe it was a drawing or a poem. God felt this way when He created the world. When the land, seas, animals, stars, and moon were all created, God looked at it all and declared that it was good. He enjoyed what He made! Then He created people and shared the world He made with them. But the people thought God's creation was missing something. Namely, they wanted to eat from the forbidden tree to see if God was keeping something from them. So they rebelled against His rules.

Their rebellion was called sin. Sin troubles God because it causes separation between Him and the people He loves. God made the world full of goodness and joy, but people brought sadness into the world when they sinned. Eventually, God decided to start over again. There was too much evil in the world. He sent a great flood to cover the earth and all its sin. Yet there was one man, Noah, who still loved and obeyed God. Oh, what joy Noah brought to God! God saved Noah, Noah's family, and a big boat full of animals from the flood.

After the flood, Noah's family sadly chose sin over God. It wasn't long before joy was missing from the earth again. God knew what to do, though. He would send His Son, Jesus, to the earth to restore the joy that once was there. Jesus would deal with the problem of sin once and for all. And where there is no sin, there is much joy! Jesus was God's ultimate plan to bring joy to the earth.

WHERE THERE IS NO SIN, THERE IS MUCH JOY!

Share about a time when you
felt really happy.
What do you think forever joy
in Jesus will feel like?

How do you think it's possible to feel joy even
when you are going through something difficult?

✚ *Ask God to help you obey Him.*

✚ *Thank God for His forgiveness of
your sins through Jesus.*

draw a picture
ABOUT WHAT YOU LEARNED TODAY

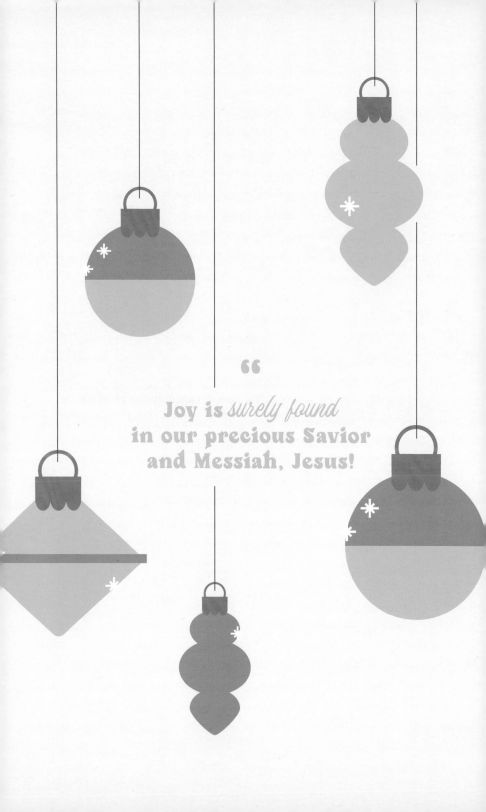

"

Joy is *surely found*
in our precious Savior
and Messiah, Jesus!

Joy
Promised

READ TOGETHER: ISAIAH 61:1-3

Have you ever heard the word "jubilee" before? A jubilee is a big party with lots of rejoicing and celebrating. In Bible times, God declared a whole year of jubilee every fifty years. During this year, people were given lots of gifts! They were released from paying back the money they owed, they were given a year of rest from their work, and they celebrated God's blessings for an entire year. It was like a vacation and party rolled into one, and it lasted for twelve whole months! Doesn't that sound fun?

This year of jubilee was a picture of the great joy Jesus would one day bring as the Savior of the world. He would cancel the debt of sin, set people free from sadness and shame, and freely give God's blessing of salvation to all who believe. Isaiah 61 describes the jubilee of the Messiah. Listen to some of the joyful words it uses: good news, liberty, freedom, favor, comfort, beauty, splendid, rebuild, restore, renew, reward, rejoice, salvation, and righteousness. Wow!

The people who heard this promise must have been bursting inside as they thought of the joys Jesus was going to bring. And Jesus did bring all of these things and more when He was born in Bethlehem. All God's promises about Jesus were true. Oh, how that makes our hearts burst within us! And even more than that, He will one day cover the entire earth with joy when He returns. Joy is surely found in our precious Savior and Messiah, Jesus!

ALL GOD'S PROMISES ABOUT JESUS WERE TRUE.

ANSWER TOGETHER

What do you think it was like for the people
who experienced living in a year of jubilee?

What joyful things have you experienced as
a result of your relationship with God?
If you don't yet have a relationship with God,
consider taking those steps toward God today.
Learn more on page 86.

PRAY TOGETHER

✚ *Thank God for being faithful to do all
He has promised.*

✚ *Ask God to help you understand the
joy He gives through Jesus.*

draw a picture

ABOUT WHAT YOU LEARNED TODAY

"
Jesus has surely
done *great things*
for us!

Joy in Jesus's Birth

READ TOGETHER: LUKE 1:44-45

When Jesus was still growing in Mary's belly, Mary visited one of her family members named Elizabeth. Elizabeth was also pregnant with a baby boy. Her baby was a miracle, too! Elizabeth was too old to have children, and her body could not grow a baby. But God helped Elizabeth and gave her a very special baby named John. When John grew up, he would encourage many people to love and obey God. He was a messenger for God and His kingdom.

When Mary visited Elizabeth, John was not yet born. But when Mary greeted Elizabeth, baby John jumped for joy right inside Elizabeth's belly! Elizabeth was filled with the Holy Spirit, and she knew Mary's baby was the most special baby of all. She rejoiced that Mary came to visit her while Jesus was growing inside of her. Elizabeth and her baby, John, were both filled with joy at the news that Jesus the Messiah was coming soon!

Mary then broke into song. She praised the Lord for all the great things He had done for her, and she praised Him for how loving and merciful He was to all His people throughout all generations. There was so much joy, so much anticipation, and so much hope in the air as Mary and Elizabeth considered the wondrous miracle of Jesus's soon arrival. And we have the same joy! Jesus's birth meant God came close to us to save us from our sin. Jesus has surely done great things for us!

JESUS'S BIRTH MEANT GOD CAME CLOSE TO US TO SAVE US FROM OUR SIN.

ANSWER TOGETHER

Read Mary's song in Luke 1:46-55.
What joyful words did you hear?

How can you share the joy of Jesus
with someone this week?

PRAY TOGETHER

✝ *Thank God for sending Jesus to save us
from our sins.*

✝ *Pray that God would help you remember
the joy Jesus gives us.*

draw a picture

ABOUT WHAT YOU LEARNED TODAY

> "
> Like Jesus, we can endure hard things while *looking forward* to the joy of what will come in eternity.

Joy in Jesus's Death and Resurrection

READ TOGETHER: HEBREWS 12:1-3

Can we remain hopeful of a future joy and be sad at the same time? Jesus shows us that the answer is yes!

Hebrews 12:1-3 says Jesus had a future joy on His mind even while He was on the cross. Can you believe that? Jesus was arrested for a crime He did not commit. He was abandoned by His friends. He was beaten and bruised. People gathered to laugh at Him while He suffered. Then, He was nailed to a cross and left to die. All of these acts He endured are horrible and very painful. But He was able to endure them because He knew the pain was only going to last a little while. Joy was coming.

Jesus died to forgive the sins of the world. His painful death had a purpose. Now, anyone who believes in Him can be forgiven of their sins and enter into a relationship with God. Even though what Jesus experienced was awful in every way, He knew joy would be the final outcome. All people who believe in Jesus have the same hope of joy! We may experience things that are unfair or painful for a while here on earth. But in eternity with Jesus, there will be no sin, no hurt, and no sadness. There will be perfect joy! Like Jesus, we can endure hard things while looking forward to the joy of what will come in eternity.

JESUS DIED TO FORGIVE THE SINS OF THE WORLD.
HIS PAINFUL DEATH HAD A PURPOSE.

ANSWER TOGETHER

What do you think heaven is like?

What is something hard or sad you are experiencing right now? Do you think this hardship will last forever?

PRAY TOGETHER

+ *Ask God to help you remember the joy of eternity.*

+ *Thank God that He is with us now in our pain and hardship.*

draw a picture
ABOUT WHAT YOU LEARNED TODAY

Advent helps us remember to _wait_ and _watch_ for this joyous day!

Joy in Jesus's Second Coming

READ TOGETHER: REVELATION 19:6-8

Do you know where Jesus is right now? After Jesus died and came back to life, He spent some time with His disciples, teaching them about what would happen next. Then, He ascended to heaven where He sat down next to God. He watches over His people and prays for them constantly from His heavenly seat.

Jesus won't be sitting next to God in heaven forever, though. He still has part of His mission to complete! One day, He will come back to earth and will get rid of all sin forever. The Bible describes Jesus's return as a big battle between Jesus and Satan. And Jesus will win! He will lock up Satan and those who follow him up so that they can never escape.

The earth will be made new and so will the heavens! God's glory will fill the whole earth in the same way water covers the wide-open ocean floors. Oceans are huge! They are deep, wide, and hold more water than we can even imagine. That is the same way the goodness of God will flood the earth when Jesus returns.

Can you imagine that? Think of what a world full of goodness, patience, mercy, wisdom, love, justice, and truth would look like. It would look like heaven on earth. Oh, what a joy that will be! All Christians really can look forward to heaven on earth becoming a reality. We do not know the day when Jesus is coming back, but we know He is coming soon. Advent helps us remember to wait and watch for this joyous day!

GOD'S GLORY WILL FILL THE WHOLE EARTH.

ANSWER TOGETHER

What problems do you have now that you
will no longer have in heaven?

*Consider how we have traced the theme of joy
throughout Scripture from Genesis to Revelation this week.*
What have you learned about God's story of joy
from studying in this way?

*Everyone who believes in Jesus and is saved from
their sin will experience the new heaven and new earth.*
Have you expressed your belief in Jesus and
asked Him to forgive your sins?
*(Parents: this would be a great time to refer to "Sharing the
Good News of the Gospel with Children" on Page 120.)*

PRAY TOGETHER

✝ *Thank God that one day He will fill the earth
with goodness and love.*

✝ *Pray that God uses you to share the good
news of Jesus with the world right now.*

draw a picture
ABOUT WHAT YOU LEARNED TODAY

Joy to the World

SUPPLIES NEEDED

Scissors
Cardstock (any color)
Glitter
Sequins
Glue
Washable paint
Paintbrushes
Sticky tack (to hang posters)

INSTRUCTIONS

In Luke 2:10-11, angels appear to shepherds to tell them about the birth of Jesus. The angels proclaim they are bringing "good news of great joy that will be for all the people." The joyous news was that the Savior had come! As Christmas approaches and we prepare to celebrate the joy of Jesus's arrival, let's proclaim joy to the world just like the angels did!

Cut out the "joy" letter templates on the next page, and trace them onto a piece of cardstock. Decorate with glitter, stickers, paint, or sequins. Let dry, then hang the joy posters around your home to remind you of the joy we have because Jesus paid the price for our sins and will come again one day to fill the whole earth with joy!

WEEK 4

Love

MEMORY VERSE

For God loved the world in this way: He gave his one and only Son, so that everyone who believes in him will not perish but have eternal life.

John 3:16

WEEK 4 - DAY 1

Read John 3:16, Romans 5:8, 1 John 4

Love

Today, we light the love candle. God is love. He created the world out of His great love and made humankind to show us His love. When sin entered the world, God's love remained. Even though sin hurts our relationship with God, God still loves us. In fact, He loves us so much that He sent His Son Jesus to forgive us of our sin. This candle reminds us of God's love that can never be extinguished. May this candle cause you to feel the warmth of God's love that shines brightly in our hearts through Jesus Christ. As you light the love candle today, read the verses above, and reflect on the love of God we see through Jesus.

PRAYER

God,

Thank You for Your amazing love. We praise You for loving us so much that You sent Jesus to die for us and give us salvation. Thank You for the gift of Jesus. We are so undeserving of Your forgiveness, but You have given it to us out of Your great love! When we feel unloved or ashamed, help us to remember and rest in the love of Christ. May we reflect Your love and share Your love with others this Advent season.

Amen.

“

Out of His *great love*
for His creation,
God put forth a plan
to *save mankind* from
the consequences of
their sin, which is death.

Love in Creation

READ TOGETHER: EPHESIANS 1:3-6

A warm embrace. Kind words. A kiss on the forehead. These are examples of how we can feel loved by others. While these actions reveal someone's love for us, the love of others is only a fraction of the amount of love God has for us.

The creation story says much about God's love. While God did not need humans, He created humans to have a relationship with Him. God created a world of abundance and invited Adam and Eve to delight in this abundance, as well as His presence with them. Adam and Eve experienced the fullness of God's love as they dwelt in the garden with Him.

However, Adam and Eve became tempted by Satan and rejected God's love by disobeying Him. Their disobedience brought sin into the world and separated them from the presence of God. The relationship between God and man was broken, but His love for them remained strong.

Out of His great love for His creation, God put forth a plan to save mankind from the consequences of their sin, which is death. John 3:16 says, "For God loved the world in this way: He gave his one and only Son, so that everyone who believes in him will not perish but have eternal life." God's love is so great that He not only put forth a plan to save us, but He sent His own Son to save us! That deep and endless love is what we remember and rejoice in this Advent season.

GOD'S LOVE IS SO GREAT THAT HE NOT ONLY PUT FORTH A PLAN TO SAVE US, BUT HE SENT HIS OWN SON TO SAVE US!

How does the creation story
speak to God's love for us?

How has God shown His love for
us through Christ?

PRAY TOGETHER

✛ *Praise God for how He never stops loving us.*

✛ *Thank God for sending Jesus out of His
great love for us.*

draw a picture
ABOUT WHAT YOU LEARNED TODAY

"

**Like a parent
rescuing their child
from the woods,
the** *pursuing love* **of
Christ chases after
us and** *saves us.*

Love Promised

READ TOGETHER: HOSEA 11:1-4, 1 JOHN 3:1

Imagine a little boy who wanders off from his mother to chase a butterfly—only to look up and realize he has become lost in the woods! But soon, his mother finds him and scoops him up into her loving arms. Each one of us is like the little boy in the woods. Our sin makes us lost and causes us to chase things we think will make us happy apart from God.

God's chosen people, the Israelites, were just like us. Even though they were God's chosen people, the Israelites often rebelled against God and went their own way. But God never stopped loving His people. The book of Hosea is a beautiful picture of God's unrelenting love. Like a loving Father, God pursued Israel and promised to rescue Israel from their rebellion, even though they turned away from Him.

When we turn to the pages of the New Testament, we see God's promise of rescue fulfilled through Jesus. Unlike Israel, Jesus was perfectly obedient to God, and Jesus's obedience led Him to die on the cross. Through His death and resurrection, Jesus's grace and forgiveness save us from the punishment of our sin. Those who come to faith in Jesus are no longer lost and wayward.

Like a parent rescuing their child from the woods, the pursuing love of Christ chases after us and saves us. Through Jesus's grace and forgiveness, we are wrapped into God's arms and declared a child of God. In Jesus, we are found and forever loved.

THOSE WHO COME TO FAITH IN JESUS ARE
NO LONGER LOST AND WAYWARD.

How is God a loving Father to us?

Even if we have been saved, we can still struggle to be obedient to God.
How does God's love for us encourage our obedience to Him?

✚ *Praise Jesus for rescuing us.*

✚ *Ask Jesus to help you remember the cost He paid on the cross so that we could be rescued.*

draw a picture
ABOUT WHAT YOU LEARNED TODAY

66

God is the *perfect*
gift-giver **because**
He has given us
Jesus Christ.

Love in the Birth of Jesus

READ TOGETHER: GALATIANS 4:4-7, EPHESIANS 2:8

What is the best Christmas gift you have ever received? While that gift is likely great, even your absolute favorite gift is not the best. Our best gift is Jesus! Often, we buy presents for others because we know they want those things. But the gift of Jesus is different. God gave us the gift of Jesus because He is what we need.

The Israelites had waited thousands of years for God to fulfill His promise to give them a Savior. When the time finally came for that Savior to come, His arrival was different from what Israel imagined. Jesus was born as a baby inside a stable of animals. His humble birth displays His humble character. In His humility, Jesus eventually laid down His life. He died on the cross so humankind could receive what we desperately need—forgiveness. Romans 6:23 says, "For the wages of sin is death, but the gift of God is eternal life in Jesus Christ our Lord." We deserve the punishment of death for our sin, but the gift of God, Jesus, saves us from this punishment.

God's love is so great that He was willing to die so we could receive the gift of salvation. God is the perfect gift-giver because He has given us Jesus Christ. When you look at the presents underneath your tree this Christmas, let them remind you of God, our giver, who gave us the best gift we could ever receive, our Savior, Jesus Christ.

GOD'S LOVE IS SO GREAT THAT HE WAS WILLING TO DIE SO WE COULD RECEIVE THE GIFT OF SALVATION.

ANSWER TOGETHER

What does it say about God's character
that He would give us Jesus?

How can we respond to what
Jesus has done for us?

PRAY TOGETHER

 *Praise God for giving us Jesus.*

*Thank Jesus for giving us the gift
of His salvation.*

draw a picture
ABOUT WHAT YOU LEARNED TODAY

"

The *gospel* is a love story that we get to *share* with the whole world, so let us share this story this *Advent* season!

Love in Jesus's Death and Resurrection

READ TOGETHER: 1 JOHN 4:7-12

We make sacrifices every day—often without knowing. Choosing to share a toy instead of keeping it all to yourself is a sacrifice. Your parents taking time off from work to care for you when you are sick is a sacrifice. These sacrifices are made out of love. When Jesus died on the cross, He sacrificed Himself because of His great love for us.

Even though God loves mankind, there is wrath between humankind and God because of our sin. When we disobey our parents, we receive a punishment because we have rebelled against them. In the same way, we all deserve punishment because of the sin we have committed against God. But Jesus stepped in to take the punishment we deserve. He took our place on the cross, sacrificing Himself, so we could be free from the punishment of our sin.

Christ's death on the cross is the greatest display of sacrificial love. Although Jesus died, He rose from the dead three days later. Jesus's death and resurrection make it possible for anyone who believes in Jesus to receive His forgiveness. His grace and forgiveness remove God's wrath and restore us to a relationship of perfect love with the Father.

We can respond to the love Christ showed us by loving others. As we make sacrifices for others, we point others to the sacrifice Jesus made for us. The gospel is a love story that we get to share with the whole world, so let us share this story this Advent season!

How can you make sacrifices
for others this week?

Why is it important that we share
Christ's love with others?

✝ *Praise Jesus for loving us so much that
He sacrificed Himself.*

✝ *Ask God for opportunities to show
sacrificial love with others this season.*

draw a picture

ABOUT WHAT YOU LEARNED TODAY

"

Jesus Christ *will* *return*, **and we will experience the fullness of His love** *forever*.

Love in the Second Coming of Jesus

READ TOGETHER: ZEPHANIAH 3:14-17

Advent is a season of waiting as we anticipate the birth of Jesus, but the Advent season also points us to the second advent, when Jesus comes again. Just as we anticipate Christmas with joy, so we are to anticipate the second coming of Jesus with joy. But why? In the Old Testament, God's people continued to disobey and rebel against Him. The more we journey through Israel's story, the more wicked we see Israel become. In the book of Zephaniah, God used a prophet named Zephaniah to warn of the judgment that would come from God if Israel did not repent.

But nestled in between the warnings of judgment is the promise of God's love. God promised to forgive His people and to give them a future of joy. This prophecy has come true, in part, because of the forgiveness we receive through Jesus, but this prophecy will fully come true when Jesus returns. At the second advent, Jesus will remove all the sin from the earth. Those who believe in Jesus will be gathered together to dwell with the Lord for all eternity. We look to this day, not in fear but with joy! Jesus Christ will return, and we will experience the fullness of His love forever.

JUST AS WE ANTICIPATE CHRISTMAS WITH JOY, SO WE ARE TO ANTICIPATE THE SECOND COMING OF JESUS WITH JOY.

Why should we look to Jesus's
second coming with joy?

*Consider how we have traced the theme of love
throughout Scripture from Genesis to Revelation this week.
What have you learned about God's story of
love from studying in this way?*

PRAY TOGETHER

✚ *Praise Jesus for giving us a reason to look
forward to His second coming.*

✚ *Pray that God will help you look to Jesus's
second coming with anticipation and joy.*

draw a picture

ABOUT WHAT YOU LEARNED TODAY

Family Activity

*Advent is a great opportunity to share the love
of Christ with others. Choose one of the ideas below,
or come up with your own ideas for how you can share
the love of Christ through action this Advent season.*

ACTIVITY IDEAS

☐ Bake cookies for a neighbor

☐ Write an encouraging letter to a family member

☐ Bring a cup of coffee to your teacher

☐ Donate some items to a local shelter

☐ Buy Christmas gifts for a family in need

Other Ideas!

- ☐ _____
- ☐ _____
- ☐ _____
- ☐ _____
- ☐ _____
- ☐ _____
- ☐ _____

FAMILY ACTIVITY FAMILY ACTIVITY FAMILY ACTIVITY FAMILY

Christmas is all about
Jesus. Come, let us
adore Him!

The Christ Candle

READ TOGETHER: LUKE 2, ISAIAH 9:6

Today, we finish lighting the Advent candles by lighting the Christ candle. The Christ candle represents the life, death, and resurrection of Jesus. On this last day, we remember and rejoice in our Savior, Jesus. We celebrate how He came to earth as a lowly baby, grew up as a sinless man, died a painful death, and rose again in victory. May this candle remind us how Jesus's grace and forgiveness wash away our sin and make us as white as snow. All of the candles we have lit this Advent season remind us how our hope, peace, joy, and love are found in Christ alone. He came to fill us with His joy, to cover us with His peace, to cleanse us with His love, and to give us a reason to hope. Christmas is all about Jesus. Come, let us adore Him!

PRAYER

God,

We praise You for who You are. We shout for joy for Your grace and faithfulness to send us Jesus. Jesus, thank You for giving us hope, peace, joy, and love. All of these gifts were bought for us through Your death and resurrection. We praise You for sacrificing Yourself so that we could be forgiven. As we reflect on Your coming, may we look to when You come again. You have saved us, You love us, and You will come back for us.

Amen

Tips for
HELPING CHILDREN MEMORIZE SCRIPTURE

The author of Proverbs writes, "Start a youth out on his way; even when he grows old he will not depart from it" (Proverbs 22:6). One of the best ways we can equip our children with the truth of the gospel—even from a very young age—is by helping them memorize Scripture.

By teaching our children to store the Word of God in their hearts, we train them in righteousness so they will become competent and equipped for every good work (2 Timothy 3:16-17). As you seek to help your children memorize Scripture, here are a few helpful tips.

- Create actions to go along with each word or phrase.

- Practice a few times a day. Some great times to practice are meals, in the car, or before bed.

- Write the first letter of each word in the verse on a post-it note, and use it as a cheat sheet until the verse is memorized.

- Post the verse in a visible place, like the bathroom mirror or on the refrigerator.

- Sing the verse to the tune of a familiar song.

- Have children look up the verse in the Bible and read it on their own.

- Keep track of verses memorized, and practice them once a week to promote long-term memory.

Sharing

THE GOOD NEWS OF THE GOSPEL
WITH CHILDREN

Many people begin their relationship with Jesus at a young age. Throughout this devotional, the good news of the gospel is presented. Children may understand their sin and need for a Savior for the first time during this Advent season. Grown-ups, you may want to ask your children if they want to make a decision to believe in Jesus and receive forgiveness for their sins. It is important not to pressure children to make this decision, but it is also important to lead them to Christ if they are ready.

When your child is ready to respond to the gospel message, there is no specific prayer to pray or formula to follow. Interestingly, the Bible never actually presents us with a prayer that leads to salvation. Instead, Jesus often calls people to believe (John 6:35) and follow Him (Matthew 19:21). The apostles teach us to "confess with your mouth, 'Jesus is Lord,' and believe in your heart that God raised him from the dead" to be saved (Romans 10:9). Scripture demonstrates that salvation is an issue of the heart. It is not the words we say but the belief in our hearts that leads to salvation. Salvation is the work of God in response to one's faith in Christ.

However, a natural overflow of believing in God is praying to Him. And what more important moment to pray to Him than the moment you realize the depth of your sin and your need for a Savior? Praying with your child in response to the gospel is meant to be a sincere conversation between a repentant sinner and a gracious God, not a script one recites to receive salvation.

Listen to your child's answers and encourage them if they say they want to repent and believe. If your child expresses their belief in Jesus and their desire to trust Him as their Savior, you may want to help them communicate their repentance and belief to God. You could lead them in a prayer that goes something like this:

> God, I've sinned against You, and I know that I can never make this right on my own. I trust that Jesus's sacrifice was enough to bring me into a real, life-changing relationship with You. Redeem my life, Lord. I cannot do it apart from You. I want to walk with You in my mind, my heart, and my actions every day, and I want to start today. Amen.

There is nothing magical about these words, nor are these words something that we pray once and then move on with our lives. They are simply communicating the admission of sin and belief in God's saving power. Salvation is an issue of the heart. This prayer begins a life-long journey of the Holy Spirit making us like Christ, and it is a journey that will find its completion on that glorious day when we finally meet Him face to face.

*Thank you for studying God's Word
with us this Advent season!*

CONNECT WITH US
@thedailygraceco
@dailygracepodcast

CONTACT US
info@thedailygraceco.com

SHARE
#thedailygraceco

VISIT US ONLINE
www.thedailygraceco.com

MORE DAILY GRACE
The Daily Grace App
Daily Grace Podcast